Edward Cooke

Arguments For and Against an Union Between Great Britain and Ireland

Edward Cooke

Arguments For and Against an Union Between Great Britain and Ireland

ISBN/EAN: 9783337322281

Printed in Europe, USA, Canada, Australia, Japan

Cover: Foto ©Suzi / pixelio.de

More available books at **www.hansebooks.com**

ARGUMENTS

FOR AND AGAINST

AN UNION,

BETWEEN

GREAT BRITAIN AND IRELAND,

CONSIDERED.

DUBLIN PRINTED: LONDON RE-PRINTED

FOR J. WRIGHT, OPPOSITE OLD BOND-STREET, PICCADILLY,

DECEMBER 1798.

ARGUMENTS

FOR AND AGAINST AN

UNION,

CONSIDERED.

IT appears from a variety of circumftances, that the fubject of incorporating the Irifh with the Britifh Legiflature, and forming a complete Union of Great Britain and Ireland, is undergoing a dufcuffion by the leading characters of both kingdoms ; and it is rumoured, that fome meafure may be propofed upon it to the two Parliaments.

The queftion is of fuch extent and importance, and applies fo warmly to all the feelings, prejudices and paffions of the human mind, that it cannot fail to be univerfally debated : the only fear is, that it will not be properly debated.

If it is to be decided by paffion, or by force, there is no mifchief which the agitation of the

queftion

queftion may not produce; if it is to be determined on its merits, it cannot fail to be ufeful. In
one cafe the rejection or adoption of it would
terminate in difcontent or convulfion; in the other,
the refult of conviction would produce fatisfaction.

The object of the confiderations which follow,
is not to give an opinion upon any Plan of Union,
which may be in contemplation, but to ftate the
general arguments which refpect the fubject, and
to prove that it ought to be difcuffed with temper,
and that it deferves fuch a difcuffion.

Let us firft view the queftion in the abftract.—
Two independent ftates, finding their feparate exiftence mutually inconvenient, propofe to form
themfelves into one ftate for their mutual benefit.

Such is the Queftion of Union, than which no
queftion can be devifed more fit for fober and
philofophical argument.

Again—Every independent fociety or ftate has
a right, confiftent with its exifting duties and
obligations, to propofe the means which appear
moft probable, for the attainment of the happinefs
of its people.

If it appears probable that fuch happinefs can
beft be attained by remaining in its prefent ftate,
feparate

feparate and independent of any other country, feparation and independency ought to be maintained at all hazards. If it appears probable, that fuch happinefs can beft be attained by a federal or an Incorporate Union with another country, fuch an Union ought to be the national object.

When the Seven United Provinces, being cruelly oppreffed by the Spanifh Government, feparated from that Government, in order to efcape from tyranny, and to fecure liberty and happinefs, they acted according to right, in declaring and eftablifh- ing their Independence.

When the Sabines found they could not maintain themfelves any longer againft the Romans, and faw, that by uniting with them, they had an opportunity of increafing their liberty, their happinefs, and their power, they acted according to the principles of reafon and right, in relinquifhing their feparate independency as a ftate, and by their Union laid the foundation of Roman greatnefs.

This reafoning and thefe inftances, form a complete anfwer to all declamation upon the common topics of national dignity and national pride. Were any perfon to exclaim, " who fhall dare to propofe, that the independence of Ireland fhall be annihilated ?" I would anfwer him by another queftion, queſtion.—If the liberty, the conveniences, the happineſs, the ſecurity of the people of Ireland, will be improved by an incorporation of the Iriſh with the Britiſh legiſlature, ſhall we not for ſuch advantages endeavour to procure that incorporation?

England was formerly divided into ſeven kingdoms, which were continually engaged in predatory wars with each other, and the iſland was a general ſcene of confuſion and barbariſm. A wiſe and ſagacious prince united theſe ſeparate kingdoms into one Empire. Did the people of the Heptarchy loſe their independence by this Union? Was a Mercian degraded by becoming an Engliſhman? Were the people of the ſeven nations made dependant, or were they debaſed and enſlaved by aboliſhing the local regulations which divided them into ſeparate and hoſtile ſocieties, deſtructive of themſelves and each other, and by aſſociating and uniting under one regimen, one code of government, and one ſovereignty?

We might extend this reaſoning, were it not too obvious, both to Wales and Scotland: How is a Welchman degraded by being repreſented in the Britiſh Parliament? How is a Scot enſlaved by becoming a Briton?

The

The question of forming an Union between two countries, must never be confused with the subjection of one country to another.—The latter is supposed to be the result of force, the former of consent; the latter is calculated to extinguish the power and independence of one of the parties; the former by the communication of privilege and the Union of strength, to increase the power and independence of both. The one is therefore, never to be submitted to, but from necessity, the other may be the object of choice.

An Union may be compared to a partnership in trade. If a merchant finds, that from circumstances of situation, want of credit or capital, he cannot carry on his business alone, with advantage, will he not be wise to unite himself, if possible, to an extensive and wealthy firm, and to become a sharer in proportion to his contribution of industry and capital, in the secure profits of an established house?

If, therefore, the measure of forming an Union between two kingdoms, whose separate existence is inconvenient, is abstractedly agreeable to reason and philosophy, and if in many instances, it has been attended with advantage to the contending parties, it is plainly a subject for temperate discussion.

If

If an Union may be advantageous, in what cafes is it likely to be moft fo?

An Union prefuppofes that when it is completed, the contracting ftates fhall be bound together by the fame Conftitution, Laws, and Government; and by an identity of interefts, and equality of privileges.

When, therefore, one of the States, defirous to form an Union, is inferior in point of civilization, agriculture, commerce, manufactures, morals, manners, eftablifhments, conftitution; and the other State is eminent and fuperior to all the world in thefe advantages; it is evident, that an Union, in fuch a cafe, muft be moft beneficial to the former—for there is every probability, that the Union will communicate, by degrees, all its advantages and excellencies; and the inferior Society will be thus. placed in a ftate of continual emulation, and improvement.

Let us compare then the fituations of Great Britain and Ireland—the former enjoys the beft practical Conftitution and Government, which any nation has ever experienced; the people. are in general the moft civilized, the moft obedient to Law, the moft honeft in dealing, the moft decent in morals, the moft regular in Religion of any

people

. people in Europe. They have the beſt agriculture, the moſt extenſive commerce, and have carried manufactures, arts, and ſciences beyond any other nation. Their ſoldiery is brave and orderly; their naval greatneſs is unrivalled.

Now, in many of theſe particulars, we acknowledge and lament the inferiority of Ireland—our civil and religious diſcontents, jealouſies and diſturbances; the conſpiracies, the inſurrections, the rebellions which have diſgraced us; proclaim our defects in civilization and policy—that the former is not ſufficiently diffuſed to prevent irregularity and licentiouſneſs, nor the latter ſtrong enough to repreſs them. Our agriculture is by no means perfect; there is only one manufacture of great importance; and commerce, though it has been of late years increaſed beyond our hopes, is not carried to that extent which the powers and reſources of the nation are able to reach.

Let theſe countries be united, and identified in government, in policy, in intereſt, what muſt be the unavoidable conſequence?—Ireland will be gradually riſing to the level of England; or England gradually ſinking to the level of Ireland; and it is obvious which is moſt probable.

If any perſon has a ſon uneducated, unimproved, and injured by bad habits, and bad company;

company; in order to remedy thefe imperfec-
tions, would it not be his firft endeavour to
eftablifh him in the beft focieties, and introduce
him into the moft virtuous, the moft polifhed,
and the moft learned company; and if he could
once reconcile him to fuch companies, and teach
him to relifh their converfation, would he not be
certain of his fon's improvement, and of his finally
turning out to his credit and fatisfaction ?

What can any fanguine Irifh Patriot wifh for
his country but that its inhabitants fhould attain
the fame habits, manners, and improvement which
make England the envy of Europe ? and by what
means can he hope to attain that end fo effectually
as by uniting with her Government, and binding up
all her interefts and concerns in the fame bottom ?

Suppofing there were no other reafons which
rendered the Union of the Sifter Kingdoms defire-
able, the ftate of Europe, and efpecially of France,
feems to dictate its peculiar policy at the prefent
day. France as not only united to herfelf, and
incorporated a great addition of territory, but has
rendered abfolutely dependent on her will, almoft
all the fmaller ftates which furround her. Geneva
is incorporated, Savoy is incorporated, all the
Auftrian provinces in Flanders, all the German
ftates, on this fide of the Rhine, are incorporated.
Spain

Spain is fubject to her influence; Holland, Switzerland, Sardinia, and the new Republic of Italy, are occupied by her armies; to every country fhe extends her principles, and her intrigues, and on this kingdom her defigns have been nearly fuccefsful. No continental power could refift her arms. Great Britain alone maintained the conteft: but, in proportion as the power of France is increafed, fo ought the ftrength of the Britifh Empire to be augmented. If, from the difunited ftate of the Britifh Empire, any particular part of it has become open to the attacks of France, or of its republican faction in England, that avenue of difunion fhould be clofed; how could it have been poffible for England to have formed the barrier, which fhe has oppofed to the French power, if Scotland as well as Ireland at this day, had continued a feparate kingdom, equally open to French intrigue? She would probably have fallen a facrifice to France, and the liberties of Europe would have fallen with her.

France well knows the principle and the force of incorporations. Every ftate which fhe unites to herfelf, fhe makes part of her empire, *cne and indivifible*, and will not fuffer any mention to be made in negotiation of reftitution. Whilft in her affected plans of policy for the liberties of the Britifh Empire, fhe maintains the principle of feparation, as effential to freedom, fhe confiders the

C   Union

Union of England and Scotland as an ufurpation of the former; and leaving England to her fate, would make Scotland and Ireland feparate Republics. France well knows the adage, *dum finguli pugnant univerfi vincuntur*; and fhe has played that game fuccefsfully; but as we wifh to check the ambition of that defperate, and unprincipled power, and if that end can only be effected by maintaining and augmenting the power of the Britifh Empire, we fhould be favourable to the principle of Union, which muft increafe and confolidate its refources.

If an Union may be defirable between two independent kingdoms, it muft be moft defirable when fuch two kingdoms are united under one Sovereign, and have feparate legiflatures; for they have all the difadvantages without the advantages of an Union. The Sovereign muft refide in one of the kingdoms: *there* would of courfe be the metropolis of the empire; *there* would be the real feat of the government; thence would flow all the counfels; and thither would refort thofe, who wifhed for favour and emolument. The kingdom, where the monarch did not refide, not having the origination of all counfels and meafures, and having much of its rents carried away by abfentees, would be in a perpetual ftate of jealoufy and difcontent; and being feparate in all refpects, but in the individual perfon of the monarch, would

would be a prey to foreign faction; and an empire thus compofed could never be in a ftate of full fecurity, for there never could be a certainty that all parts of it would purfue the fame fyftem.

The objections to this predicament were fo ftrong in Scotland before the Union, that the Scots brought in a Bill of Settlement, to provide that their Monarch fhould never be the fame perfon as the King of England; upon this the alternative of Union or Separation became inevitable, and at length they wifely preferred the former—What has been the confequence ? The Scotch, becoming entitled to all the privileges of Britifh fubjects, have greatly added to their own civilization and wealth : have enjoyed internal tranquillity and fecurity; and enabled Great Britain, by the confolidation of the whole ifland under one Government, to reach that height of profperity and glory which makes her the envy and the protectrefs of Europe.

In the fituation which Scotland held previous to the Union does Ireland ftand at prefent; except that the Crown of Ireland is by exprefs ftatutes of declaration and recognition perpetually annexed to and dependant upon the Crown of England; fo that whoever is King of England, is in right of that title, *ipfo facto*, King of Ireland. The King of Ireland, as the King of Scotland before the Union, refides in another kingdom. The counfels for

the

the Government of Ireland are framed in the British Cabinet ; the Government of Ireland is actually adminiftered by a British Lord Lieutenant, who diftributes the patronage of the Crown ; the Irish Parliament is fuppofed to be in a great degree fubject to British influence, and near one million of the rents of the kingdom are annually exported to Abfentees. The jealoufies upon thefe points are great and unavoidable, and form the perpetual topic for inflaming the minds of the people in newfpapers, and the unvarying theme of complaint and invective by Parliamentary Oppofition. Nor can this inconvenience ceafe whilft affairs remain as at prefent ; for fo long as we form part of the British Empire, we muft acknowledge one Executive Power, one prefiding Cabinet ; and it is of indifpenfable neceffity for that Cabinet to induce every part of the empire to purfue the fame principles of action, and to adopt the fame fyftem of meafures, as far as poffible : and as the interefts of England muft ever preponderate, a preference will be always given to her, or fuppofed to be given, which has the fame effect. The Irish Parliament is certainly in its inftitution independent ; it may when it pleafes act contrary to the policy of the empire ; it may exhort the King to make war when the views of England are pacific ; it may declare againft a war when England is driven into one by neceffity ; and it has actually afferted a Right to chufe a Regent of its own appointment,

diftinct

diftinct from the Regent of Great Britain; it may also declare againft treaties, and refufe to ratify commercial articles. Now if Ireland, having thefe powers, fhould at any time exert them in oppofition to the conduct of England, the empire would be endangered or diffolved; and fo long as the Parliament of Ireland, from motives of difcretion and prudence, does not exert them, it will be fubject to the imputation of being meanly and corruptly fubfervient to the Britifh Cabinet; and the imputation being conftantly repeated and always liable to be renewed, will have in future, as it has had already, a prejudicial influence on the public mind, leading the people to diftruft and to difparage their legiflature.

Add to this the melancholy reflection, that the Irifh Parliament has been long made the Theatre for Britifh Faction. When at a lofs for fubjects of grievance in Great Britain, they ever turn their eyes to this kingdom, in the kind hope that any feed of difcontent may be nourifhed, by their foftering attention, into ftrength and maturity.— Incapable of beating the minifter on his own ground, they change the place of attack, and wound him from the fide of Ireland. Need I allude to the Queftion of the Commercial Propofitions, the Queftion of the Regency, and the Queftion of the Catholics; when we have feen the Leaders of the Britifh Oppofition come forward

to

to fupport the Character of Irifh Rebels, to palliate
and to juftify Irifh Treafon, and almoft to vindi-
cate Irifh Rebellion? If then, differing from Great
Britain in Imperial Queftions, would diffolve the
Empire, and if uniformly concurring with her,
muft fubject the Parliament to perpetual imputation of criminal fubferviency to a foreign Cabinet;
and if fo long as an Irifh free and independent
Parliament remains, it muft be fubject to the
Cabals of Britifh Party; might it not be a meafure
of wifdom to incorporate the Parliaments together, and that Ireland fhould accept the fame
Guarantee for its Liberty and Profperity, as fatis-
fies the people of England?

It is notorious that before the Union, Scotland had always a connexion and alliance with
France; which fince the Union has totally va-
nifhed. Her feelings, conduct and policy have,
fince that period, been entirely Britifh. It is equally
notorious that a correfpondence was kept up with
France, by a party in this kingdom, efpecially
fo long as the Pretender lived, who had the
appointment to all the Irifh Roman Catholic
Bifhoprics, and who difpofed of them in concert
with the Court of France. It is alfo manifeft that
a connexion with France has been lately renewed
upon new principles; and it is obvious that the
French will never ceafe to intrigue in this kingdom,
whilft we remain in our prefent ftate, which pre-
fents

fents fo favourable an opening to intrigue of every kind.

Now let us fuppofe that an Union of the Britifh and Irifh Legiflatures were completed upon fair and equitable principles, what would be our new fituation? The Monarch would remain in England as at prefent; the Abfentee proprietors of land might in fome degree increafe ; and London, as at prefent, would be the general refort for bufinefs, for advancement, for pleafure. But the Britifh Cabinet would receive a mixture of Irifhmen, and the counfels of the Britifh Parliament would be much influenced by the weight and ability of the Irifh Members ; all our party contefts would be transferred to Great Britain; Britifh faction would ceafe to operate here; there would be no jealoufy of Britifh Influence on the Cabinet or Parliament ; there would be no clafhing of diftinct interefts, no fear of Ireland becoming too powerful to govern. France could no longer fpeculate on the nature of our diftinct Government and Parliament ; and hope to feparate the kingdom, in fact, from Great Britain, as it is already feparated in theory. The cultivation, the improvement of Ireland, like that of Scotland, would be peculiarly attended to, as the increafe of our wealth, confequence, ability, and power, muft tend to increafe the fecurity of the Empire, not to endanger it; and in pro- portion that we felt the benefit of an Union, our attachment to it would be ftrengthened.

All

All writers have agreed in condemning what is called *imperium in imperio*. It is this vice of conftitution which has annihilated Poland, where every fenator was a fovereign; and has enflaved the Seven United Provinces, where each province was a Sovereign. Franklin and Wafhington, the founders of the American Empire, had not courage in their firft project of a conftitution for the American ftates, to exclude this radical evil, but left each ftate independent. So foon as the preffure of neceffity, which had confederated the ftates, ceafed in confequence of peace, the fault of fuch a conftitution became evident: it was clear to men of common capacity, that an empire, confifting of Thirteen independent focieties, without one common Imperial controul, would foon divide into Thirteen independent empires. To obviate this neceffary, though poffibly diftant confequence, the wifdom of the Americans projected a new conftitution, in which this original vice was remedied; the feparate independency of each ftate was wifely relinquifhed; a general legiflative, and a general executive were formed for the government of the Union in every imperial concern; and each refpective ftate was confined to local and municipal objects. At the fame time, a juft deference was paid to all the Teft Laws and religious eftablifhments throughout the Union; and each ftate being allowed to maintain its ecclefiaftical arrangements, all religious ftruggle and animofity was prevented.

To

To the wifdom of this plan of Union the ftrength
. and happinefs of the United States may be attri-
buted—If each: had retained to itfelf its feparate
independent Legiflature, is it probable that the
American Empire could have lafted to the prefent
day? If French intrigue had at one time fuch influence in América as nearly to have overturned the
exifting Union, how could its efforts have been
refifted, when the gaining of one ftate alone might
have diffolved the Union? To injure America in
its prefent form, a majority of the reprefentatives
of the whole Union muft be feduced; to have
deftroyed her power under her firft Conftitution,
the corruption of one ftate alone would have been
fufficient.

What are the fentiments of Mr. Adams, the
Prefident of the United States, with refpect to
their firft federal and the prefent incorporate
Union—" The former," fays he, " was formed
" upon the model and example of all the con-
" federacies, ancient and modern, in which the
" federal council was only a diplomatic body;
" even the Lycian, which is thought to have been
" the beft, was no more. The magnitude of
" territory, the population, the wealth and com-
" merce, and efpecially the rapid growth of the
" United States, have fhewn fuch a government
" to be inadequate for their wants; and the new
" fyftem, which feems admirably calculated to

D   " *unite*

" *unite* their interefts and affections, and bring
" them to an uniformity of principles and fenti-
" ments, is equally well combined to unite their
" wills and forces as a fingle nation. A refult of
" accommodation cannot be fuppofed to reach the
" perfection of any one : but the conception of
" fuch an idea, and the deliberate Union of fo
" great and various a people, in fuch a plan, is
" without all partiality or prejudice, if not the
" greateft exertion of human underftanding, the
" greateft fingle effort of rational deliberation which
" the world has ever feen."

If fuch are the fentiments of the prefent, let us
advert to the opinions of their late Prefident,
General Wafhington. In the letter addreffing the
prefent conftitution of America for acceptation,
he has thefe words—" In all our deliberations upon
" this fubject, we kept fteadily in our view, that
" which appears to us the greateft intereft of every
" true American, *the confolidation of our union,*
" in which is involved our property, fafety, per-
" haps our national exiftence. This important
" confideration, ferioufly and deeply impreffed upon
" our minds, led each ftate in the convention to be
" lefs rigid in points of inferior magnitude, than
" might have been otherwife expected ; and thus
" the conftitution, which we now prefent, is the
" refult of a fpirit of amity, and of that mutual
                                    " deference

" deference and conceffion, which the peculiarity
" of our political fituation rendered indifpen-
" fable."

When, therefore, an Union is propofed to our
confideration, it may not be prudent for us to fpurn
at a principle, which the fagacity of Adams, and
the virtue of Wafhington, confidered as indifpenfable to the profperity, fafety, and perhaps the
exiftence of America; a principle, which has dif-
appointed the prophecy of politicians, that the
American Union would fplit into feparate and con-
temptible ftates, which has preferved her from the
intrigue and corruptions and infolence of France;
and which enables her to defy the menaces of that
unprincipled power, with confcious fuperiority.

Having confidered a few general topics, which
the quftion of Union naturally fuggefts, let us
examine the arguments which refult from the particular fituation of Ireland, as to its property,
its eftablifhments, and religious divifions.

Nine-tenths of the property of Ireland are in
poffeffion of Britifh Defcendants. Their lands
were taken from the original inhabitants, and con-
firmed to the prefent poffeffors, chiefly by the Act
of Settlement, but a large part of them was held
under Britifh Acts of Parliament for a century.
The poffeffors of thefe lands are of the Proteftant
religion,

religion, and acknowledge the King as the head of their church; whereas the original inhabitants are Catholics, and acknowledge the spiritual jurisdiction of a foreign power. These Protestants, thus possessing nine-tenths of the property, are only one-fourth of the inhabitants in number, and they have been obliged to rely upon British assistance, for the preservation of their property and existence at different periods.

The established Religion is the Protestant, and the Church is, in Constitution, similar to that of England, and endowed with the Tythes of the whole kingdom, and with great property in land. The Pastors of the dissenting Protestants are in a degree supported by grants of the Legislature.

The Catholics having shewn great power in the contest at the Revolution, were long subjected to a severe code of laws, which kept them in subordination; that code has, within these few years, been almost entirely repealed; but, though they enjoy a complete toleration, they are by no means contented, but demand political equality with the Protestants, and such an alteration in the Parliamentary Constitution, as will give their numbers proportionate power.

The Protestants, recollecting the struggles which were made by the Catholics in the reign of Elizabeth,

Elizabeth, in the reign of Charles the Firſt, and in the reign of James the Second, and poſſibly fancying that they diſcover ſimilar views in the preſent unhappy conteſt, act with diſtruſt and caution. They plauſibly argue, that thoſe who have the ſuperiority of number, when once they can obtain the power, will not long want the property of the ſtate. They guard therefore with vigilance their Eccleſiaſtical and Parliamentary Eſtabliſhments, and look to Great Britain as the guarantee of their ſafety and importance.

The Proteſtants ſtate, that when the Catholics were reſtrained by ſevere laws, the kingdom continued in tranquillity for a century ; but ſo ſoon as national confidence, the reſult of that tranquillity, induced them to repeal the Reſtrictions by which the Catholics were bound, the ancient ſpirit of rivalry revived, and the Catholics demanded ſuch a change of the Conſtitution, as would gradually transfer to them all the power of the ſtate.

The Proteſtants feel likewiſe other cauſes of diſtruſt, ſuggeſted by recent circumſtances, on which it is deſirable to caſt a veil, when accuſation on one ſide, and juſtification on the other, tend more to exaſperate than to conciliate, and to prolong our diſtractions than heal them.

Would to God it were poſſible to bury all that has paſſed in benevolent oblivion ; but ſuch a con-
ſummation,

fummation, though devoutly wifhed, cannot be fuddenly expected. Whilft the opinions of Europe are afloat; when all the foundations of fociety are, as it were, broken up and torn afunder; when all the old principles and notions, which bound us together in fubordination and peace, are loofened or diffolved; when it appears dubious and uncertain what turn the public mind will affume, and in what fyftem it will ultimately repofe; the expectation of any quick return to former difpofitions of confidence, and habits of amity are poffibly chimerical.

In the mean while, under the prefent temper and feelings, it is not to be hoped that Proteftants will confent to furrender their political powers, much lefs can they be perfuaded, that they could do it with fafety.

At the fame time, whilft Ireland continues a feparate kingdom, the Catholics will not drop their claims, nor the argument of numbers in their favour. So far from dropping their claims, they have already renewed them; and the Catholics of Waterford, in an addrefs to the Lord Lieutenant, have repeated their demand for political equality, and advanced it on a plea of merit. They have ftill, and will ever have electioneering partifans in parliament, and fpeculative advocates

advocates in England to feed their hopes, and they will be fupported by every open oppofer, or fecret ill-wifher to the government.

If then the feparate Conftitution and Eftablifhments, and Teft Laws of Ireland are to continue as at prefent, the kingdom muft remain in a continual ftate of irritation—the numbers of Catholics compared to Proteftants are as three to one. Modern political writers upon Religious Eftablifhments lay it down as a principle, that every ftate ought to eftablifh that religious fect which is moft numerous; but as it happens that in Ireland, the moft numerous religious fect does not acknowledge the fupremacy of the ftate, but profeffes itfelf to be fubject to a foreign jurifdiction; their religion could not be eftablifhed, without deftroying the Conftitution, which is founded on the principles of Civil and Ecclefiaftical Liberty, and the Exclufion of foreign interference and jurifdiction.

But fuppofe, at length, that the Proteftants, worn out by importunity, concede to the demand of political Equality made by the Catholics— what are the confequences?

In the firft place, the prefent Parliamentary Teft Oaths muft be repealed, and a new Oath framed to meet Catholic Feelings, and admit the jurifdiction of the Pope.

5

In

In the fecond place, the Act of Supremacy and of Uniformity, muft be repealed. For nothing could be fo abfurd, as to make men who deny the fupremacy of the King, and the competency of Parliament in Ecclefiaftical Concerns, members of the fupreme power, viz. the Legiflature; and at the fame time, to fubject thefe very men to the penalties of Premunire and Treafon for denying that fupremacy and competency.

In the third place, you eftablifh the principle, that the ftate is indifferent in religious concerns, and that it is of no confequence to the ftate, what is the religion of its fubjects; from which it follows, either that there ought to be no eftablifhed religion, at all, but that religion fhould be left to chance—or fecondly, that all religions fhould be equally eftablifhed—or thirdly, that if one is to be eftablifhed for the fake of religious inftruction, it ought to be the religion of the majority, which is the Catholic.

In the fourth place, you eftablifh, or acquiefce in the right of the Pope to a real, and effential jurifdiction within this realm, in all matters relating to the Church and its Government; and the right which has been afferted of the College of Cardinals, which is the Pope's Cabinet, to manage the ecclefiaftical affairs of Ireland.

Thus

Thus so soon as the Catholics of Ireland are admitted into the Legislature, and the Test Oaths and Act of Supremacy repealed, the Protestant Church Establishment becomes a public wrong. That Establishment is defensible at present, because, on principles of reason, and from the nature of a free constitution, no religious sect can claim a right to be established and supported by the state which denies the competency of the state to regulate their conduct; but when that principle is abandoned, the defence of the Protestant Church Establishment is abandoned also.

It further follows, from the admission of the Catholics to political equality, that the frame of the House of Commons should be reformed. It is a known historical fact, that the Irish House of Commons was framed with the sole view of excluding Roman Catholics; when therefore the principle of excluding Roman Catholics is given up, the alteration of the House of Commons in favour of the Catholics follows of course.

Admitting the Catholics to seats in the Legislature, and retaining the present Parliamentary Constitution, would be like inviting a man to dinner, and on his acceptance of the invitation, shutting the door in his face.

If then Reform must follow what is called Emancipation, and one be the unavoidable conse-

quence

quence of the other, would not a revolution of power foon take place? would it not pafs from Proteftant into Catholic hands? and what hope could the Proteftants retain of preferving their fituation when they had loft their power in the Legiflature, and their right to the Church Eftablifhment.

Let us confider then what would be the natural effects of a favourable Legiflative Union.

Firft—The empire would have but one Legiflature, one organ of the public will, and the dangers which arife from an *imperium in imperio*, from two fupreme powers would be avoided.

Secondly—Ireland would be in a *natural* fituation; for all the Proteftants of the empire being united, fhe would have the proportion of fourteen to three in favour of her eftablifhment; whereas at prefent there is a proportion of three to one againft it.

Thirdly—The Catholics would lofe the advantage of the argument of numbers, which they at prefent enjoy, and the Conftitution of the Empire would agree with the theory.

Fourthly—Whilft Ireland remains a. feparate Country from Great Britain, Great Britain is not

pledged

pledged upon any fpecific principle to fupport one feƈt in Ireland more than another; if fhe cannot preferve the connexion of the two kingdoms by upholding the Proteftants in their eftablifhment, their power, and their property, I know not by what tie fhe is debarred from affifting the Catholics; for whilft the kingdoms are feparate and independent, Ireland, except where the Crown is concerned, is merely bound by the ties of intereft to England, and in a fimilar manner England is only bound by the Rights of the Crown and ties of intereft to Ireland. She is pledged to preferve Ireland to the Britifh Crown, but not to any particular means or any particular principles for maintaining that connexion. But if Ireland was once united to Great Britain by a Legiflative Union, and the maintenance of the Proteftant Eftablifhment were made a fundamental article of that Union, then the whole Power of the Empire would be pledged to the Church Eftablifhment of Ireland, and the property of the whole Empire would be pledged in fupport of the property of every part.

An objeƈtion to this reafoning has been made by ftating that an Union would encreafe Abfentee Proprietors; that the proprietors of eftates are generally Proteftants; that of courfe Proteftant influence would decreafe, and confequently the fecurity for Proteftant property.

The

The anfwer to this objeƈion is, that it does not appear that the Abfentees from Scotland increafed after the Union, and that an argument from experience in political reafoning is fuperior to any argument in theory. Another mode of reply is, that fuppofe Abfentees were to be increafed, this evil would be compenfated by the folid advantage of having a fixed unalterable Conftitution, and of having the whole power and property of Great Britain its guarantees. When once the hope of change were at an end, and the hope of forcing fuch a change deftroyed, diffatisfaƈion would fink into acquiefcence, and acquiefcence foften into content.

Another objeƈion is, that if an Union be made upon Proteftant Principles, it cannot fail to excite the oppofition of the Catholics, and to encreafe their difaffeƈion to a Government which perpetually bars them from power; that confequently the Catholics would be more and more difpofed to cultivate a foreign conneƈion, and when free from the vigilance of a Proteftant Refident Parliament, more likely to effeƈuate that conneƈion, and the plans refulting from it, without being deteƈed.

To folve this objeƈion it is only neceffary to ftate it as a *petitio principie.* What ground is there to affume that the Catholics will affume an Union, though founded on Proteftant Principles?

Why

Why may not an Union be fo fhaped as to be favourable to the Proteftants, without being unfavourable to the Catholics?

Firft—A Free Toleration will be fecured to their Religion. Their power of electing Reprefentatives will be perpetuated, as well as their capacity of filling moft of the offices of State.

Second—It may be advifeable to connect with an Union a proper fupport for their Clergy and fome fyftem of regulation for their Church, not inconfiftent with their Ecclefiaftical Principles, and calculated to do away mifconceptions of their religious tenets, and to difcontinue practices which have been attended with inconvenience.

Third—The difpenfations which arife in counties from Candidates ftanding on the Proteftant or Catholic interefts, and all little parifh jealoufies will ceafe, from which circumftance great inconveniences have been already felt.

Fourth—If the Proteftant Intereft be fecured, there will be no neceffary ftate partiality towards Proteftants, which is a natural fource of complaint.

Fifth—Catholics will feel more confident under a Legiflature framed upon a more extended bafis,
where

where the majority of members will not be influenced againſt them by local prejudices or antipathies.

Sixth—Sectarian ſtruggle will terminate, and
tranquillity being reſtored, animoſities will gradually relax, and there being no ground for political
jealouſy and contention, the habits and connections
of ſocial life will re-produce confidence and friend-
ſhips, where exiſt, at preſent, rivalry and ſuſpicion.

Seventh—An opening may be left in any plan
of Union, for the future admiſſion of Catholics to
additional privileges. And Proteſtants can never
object to ſuch an opening, as they may reſt aſ-
ſured, that the Britiſh Proteſtant Parliament will
not imprudently admit Catholic pretenſions, as
the Teſt Laws could not be partially repealed;
and it is evident, that the Catholics could not
force their claims with hoſtility againſt the whole
power of Great Britain and Ireland.

Eighth—The Catholics aremoſt numerous in the
ſouth and weſt of Ireland; and it is conceived,
that thoſe parts of the kingdom would be moſt
benefited by an Union, as to agricultural and
commercial advantages.

Ninth—As all the ſtruggles of the Catholics for
political predominancy have failed, and as they
cannot hope to carry their wiſhes by domeſtic or
even

even foreign force, they would do well to adopt a
fettlement, which would enfure them many political and all civil advantages, and reft fatisfied
with a much greater degree of toleration than
Proteftants have ever enjoyed under a Catholic
ftate.

To anfwer the other objection which was
ftated, we may obferve, it does not follow that, if
an Union were made, that the government of Ireland would be lefs vigilantly adminiftered; it
probably would be adminiftered with more attention; becaufe it would be lefs diftracted by the
bufinefs of party and of Parliament; and for the
fame reafons, it would be adminiftered more im-
partially.

With regard to Diffenters, they are fuppofed to
be in a ratio of about one-feventh to the whole
population of the kingdom, and of one-fixth to
the Catholics. They are moftly manufacturers,
and fome of them are merchants; but they have
little influence in the prefent reprefentation.

Whilft Ireland remains a feparate kingdom, they
are the leaft confiderable body of the people; but
were an Union formed with Great Britain, the
Diffenting intereft would be in a very different
ratio in the empire, and their importance and
power would proportionably rife.

It

It is difficult to comprehend the wifdom of their junction with the Catholics, in order to overthrow the Proteftant power and eftablifhment; for, fuppofing their project to have been completed, they would have been at the mercy of their allies.

If they had fucceeded in their plans with the Catholics, their confequence in the ftate would have been probably annihilated; if an Union takes place, their importance in the empire will encreafe; and, as to their ftaple manufacture, it will be fecured for ever.

As it is probable that a modus for Tythes will accompany the meafure of an Union, both Catholics and Diffenters would be effentially relieved and benefited by that part of a new fyftem.

Some perfons have conceived that it might be advantageous to the Diffenters, if the government of their Church were more affimilated to the Church of Scotland, which is under the moft excellent difcipline; but when the ftumbling block of Tythes is removed, they may probably fall in with the Proteftant Church. The caufe of difference between Proteftants and Diffenters have been for fome time obfolete, and they refort to feparate congregations, more from early prejudice and cuftom, than from any rational or even alledged neceffity.

Having

Having considered briefly in what manner an Union would affect the great religious descriptions of the people, we may proceed to examine its influence on the different orders and classes of the State.

The Peerage would probably in any plan of Union, be reprefented like the Scotch peers, by a delegation to the British Parliament. This arrangement would not affect those nobles who are peers of Great Britain, and it would be favourable to those who refide in Great Britain. There are forty-one of the former clafs, and about eighty of the latter. The remaining fourfcore peers who attend Parliament occafionally, would be the only peers materially interefted, but almoft all of them have confiderable property in land, and as all perfonal privileges and prerogatives would remain to them, the general advantages of an Union in giving permanent fecurity to their titles and their properties, would compenfate any diminution of confequence they might feel from their not being all certain of feats in the British Parliament.

The fpiritual peers would be amply recompenfed by the fecurity given to their diocefan eftates, and to the general interefts and eftablifhments of the church.

F   The

The fame reafoning will apply to thofe who have parliamentary influence in the Houfe of Commons: Yet it muft be acknowledged that fome facrifices muft be made of power, of emolument, of importance. Many fchemes have been in circulation for adjufting the reprefentation of this kingdom in the Britifh Parliament. It is not the defign of this publication to examine them; but can it be doubted that a reafonable reprefentation may be felected, which, however, it muft interfere with the conveniencies of fome individuals, will give this kingdom a proportionate influence in the Houfe of Commons of the empire. There is no difficulty in the fubject fo great, which may not be obviated, if an Union is of importance to be attained, and if we ferioufly endeavour to effect it.

The chief oppofition to the meafure, muft be expected from the Bar, who are fuppofed to be more perfonally interefted againft it than any clafs in fociety. It is a general habit in the gentlemen of Ireland to educate their fons at the Temple, and the number of barrifters is much greater in proportion here than in England. And as the profeffion will not fupport, by any means, the numbers which purfue it, lawyers in Ireland extend their circle to politics, and are very numerous in Parliament, and extremely active in the bufinefs of it. In England there are few lawyers in the

Houfe

Houfe of Commons; whereas in Ireland they are a formidable phalanx. Were a legiflative Union to take place, Irifh lawyers would be deprived of the parliamentary market for their abilities and ambition; they could not attend the Britifh Parliament without renouncing bufinefs; they would be entirely confined to profeffional profpects; and mere political emoluments and fituations, would be taken from their grafp.

But when oppofition to an Union came forward from the Bar, it muft be taken into confideration, that the very reafons which make the Bar oppofe an Union, are arguments in favour of it.

1. It is obvioufly the intereft of the nation, that the law fhould be accurately and deeply ftudied; and it will be more probable that ftudents will pay attention to their profeffion when their hopes of advancement are confined to knowledge and ability in the line of it. In proportion as you have abler lawyers, you will have abler judges, efpecially when the temptation of placing them upon the bench, from political reafons, is removed.

2. It is obvious that it would be prudent to exclude from the Legiflature, young adventurers, who have but little ftake in the country, who have acquired by habit a facility of fpeaking upon every fubject, and upon every fide of a fubject, and who

who only confiders a feat in Parliament as the means of bringing their abilities to market.

It does not, however, appear that the profpects of the Bar would be materially injured by an Union; the offices to which lawyers are ufually appointed, would remain the fame; and if the road to them was more through profeffional merit, than Parliamentary fervices, it does not appear, that either the Bar or the Public would be injured.

It is faid, alfo, that the oppofition of the Bar is not likely to be unanimous, and that fome leading characters, who have thought moft on the fubject, and who are capable of thinking beft, who ought to have great weight, where their intereft is in no fhape concerned, and where purfuit of public good can alone fway their opinions, fo far from confidering an Union as deftructive, conceive it as pregnant with folid and permanent benefit. Aged and experienced characters are certainly as liable to political temptations, as the virtuous ardency of youth; but where no private intereft can operate, and efpecially where the point of intereft, the *cui bono*, lies againft an opinion given, one fhould never hefitate between the natural precipitation of youth, and the cautious decifions of experience.

To

To demonſtrate to the Clergy, the advantages
of an Union, would be loſt labour indeed; if
they are ſuppoſed in general to be ſufficiently
ſenſible to the intereſts of the Church, we may
ſafely leave them to their uſual diſcernment, in
the queſtion before us.

The gentlemen of landed property, would be
merely affected, as the proſperity of the kingdom in general would be increaſed or diminiſhed.
If an Union would produce tranquillity, ſecurity,
commercial and agricultural advantages, eſtates
in lands would be proportionably benefited.
Political conteſts, party ſtruggles may be the
harveſt of enterprizing adventurers, but they blight
the hopes, and blaſt the fortunes of country
gentlemen. Land in England, during times of
peace, is ſold from thirty to forty years purchaſe;
in Ireland the price of land ſeldom exceeds twenty
years purchaſe. This is attributable to the ſuppoſed different ſtate of tranquillity and ſecurity of
the two kingdoms. The continual inſurrections in
different parts of the country, of White Boys, Oak
Boys, Right Boys, Defenders, United Iriſhmen,
have made reſidence unſafe, and diminiſhed the
certainty of rents, and the value of tenure. If it
is probable that an Union would put an end to
theſe diſorders, by introducing ſteadineſs of adminiſtration, and regular ſubordination, the value
of eſtates would gradually riſe to the Engliſh level,
and

and fpeculators in land, would naturally prefer this kingdom as the fcene of improvement and experiment in proportion as the foil is in general fuperior to that of England, and from being lefs improved, more fit for experiment. The monied capital of England, has of late years been increafed to fuch a degree, that, notwithftanding the enormous loans which have been borrowed by Government; the monied men are embarraffed in what manner to inveft the capitals with advantage and fecurity. When a peace arrives, and loans fhall ceafe; the difficulty of employing capital will be augmented, and there can be no doubt that if the ftate of this country can be rendered fecure, it will be abundantly employed in Irifh purchafes and Irifh fpeculation.

It is alfo certain, that Great Britain does not produce fufficient corn for her confumption; it muft be a great object, therefore, for Irifh landed gentlemen to fecure a preference in the Britifh market for ever, which an Union would certainly effect.

As we fuppofe the Union which we are difcuffing, will confer all commercial advantages which Great Britain enjoys upon Irifh fubjects, it would be loft time to prove that our merchants muft be gainers by the meafure. The Britifh adminiftration, in order to encreafe the wealth of the kingdom, for the purpofes of power, are perpetually employed
in

in devifing the means of extending the commerce of England; and under the wife regulations of that Government, a commerce has been eftablifhed; and by the late naval victories has been fecured, which is the aftonifhment of the world. An Union then will place the Irifh merchant upon an equality with the Britifh, and he will be certain to enjoy for ever the fame privileges, protection, regulations, bounties and encouragements, as are enjoyed by the greateft commercial country that ever flourifhed.

The queftion of Union will be debated in the metropolis, and one of the chief arguments againft it is, that it will ruin the metropolis, and render it a defert. The fame argument was ufed moft powerfully at the time of the Scotch Union, with regard to Edinburgh: the defertion of that capital, was predicted, the bankruptcy of its fhopkeepers, the ruin of its proprietors, was foretold and infifted upon; yet, notwithftanding the Union, and the prophecy, Edinburgh, fo far from decaying, has flourifhed more fince the Union, than it had done before. It will be confidered, that Dublin *muft* ftill be the refidence of a Viceroy and his court; that fciences, arts, amufements, may be culti- vated in proportion, as there will be lefs atten- tion to politics; that it will be the feat of juftice, which will be adminiftered as at prefent; the chief feat of revenue, and the head-quarters of the army. It will probably monopolize the corn

7

trade

trade between Great Britain and Ireland; and from the circumftance of the Canals, which are making in every part of England, and communicating with London, its commerce for all Englifh goods with Liverpool, will greatly increafe; and in proportion, as canals from Dublin are carried to different parts of the kingdom, it will be the depot for their confumption in all articles of Britifh manufacture and import.

A fimilar prediction is made as to the depopulation of the country in general; and with much lefs reafon. For what induces refidence? Is it not peace and comfort, and fecurity? What has banifhed fo many families, but the lofs of thefe invaluable bleffings? Reftore to Ireland good humour and tranquillity, and comfort, and fecurity; her fugitives will foon return, taxes will be lower in Ireland, living will be cheaper. Thefe advantages, affifted by the natural attraction of property, and the place of nativity, will foon bring back the proprietors of the foil. Property is ever fluctuating; men of eftate are apt to be imprudent and prodigal; and the accumulations of wealth, acquired by the lawyer, the merchant, the manufacturer, and the farmer, are ultimately invefted in the purchafe of land. New purchafers do not early abandon their property; as, therefore the wealth and trade of the country encreafe, the purchafers of land will encreafe, and with new purchafers new refidents.   The

The adverfaries of an Union admit, that it will be beneficial to trade and manufactures; we need not then be terrified by alarms of depopulation.

The next city in confequence to the metropolis is Cork, which enjoys a fituation particularly calculated for foreign trade, and an excellent harbour for Men of War to refort to for the protection of the ifland and its commerce. It is alfo the emporium of provifions for the Britifh Navy, and a place for all homeward bound convoys to make to in times of war, when the channel might be dangerous to approach. From the convenience of the fituation of Cork, it would probably, after an Union, become a Marine Station, and a Dock-yard would be there formed. It is known that the three prefent harbours of England, viz. the Thames, Portfmouth, and Plymouth, are inadequate to the extent of the navy; and that a new ftation is greatly wanted. If an Union were once effected, there can be little doubt that Cork would be felected for the purpofe.

Limerick and Waterford would not be particularly affected, except in proportion as an Union, by inducing the import of Britifh capital, and the general extenfion of trade, fhould naturally augment their commercial exertions; and this general argument is applicable to all parts of the South-weft.

G

With

With regard to the North of Ireland, which carries on a manufacture of linen, of which 52,000,000 of yards have been exported in one year; all that can be defired is to confirm a trade, which, by its extent, feems a monopoly.. Great Britain gives a preference in her market, to Irifh over German linens of 37 per cent. and grants a bounty of three half-pence a yard on all Irifh linens re-exported, the value of which does not exceed eighteen-pence a yard. Thefe advantages in favour of the North of Ireland, England might repeal or diminifh, whenever fhe pleafes; by an Union, they might be fixed for ever.

It may now be defirable to obviate feveral objections which are naturally and generally brought forward to diffuade Ireland from an Union.

Firft.—*An Union would extinguifh Ireland.* The name may remain, and furely it will not extinguifh the people and the foil; though it may meliorate both. If its reprefentatives fit in the fame place with its Executive, and by that means obtain great influence in the councils of the Empire; and the fame fecurity for its fituation as the people of England enjoy, how will Ireland be extinguifhed?

Second.

Second.—What can be such madness and folly as for a people to send its Legislature from the Metropolis of their own Country, which is convenient to all its Members, to sit in the Metropolis of another Country, separated by the sea, at a great distance, to the inconvenience of all its Members?

The answer to this objection is, that Ireland is part of an Empire; that the King of Ireland resides in that distant Metropolis; that having two Legislatures in one Empire is incompatible with its safety; that a Consolidation of those Legislatures promises great advantages; that the distance of Ireland from the Metropolis of England, is not greater than that of Scotland; that in the French Republic the distance of Toulon and many other parts from Paris, is much greater than the distance of Dublin from London; and that in America the distance of Charlestown and other Capitals from Philadelphia, is in the same proportion: yet no inconvenience is felt in these cases; and the inconvenience of distance may be easily balanced by the advantages of Union.

Third.—Shall we tamely resign that Legislature whose Independence was so gloriously asserted and established by the arms of the Volunteers?

It is not intended to detract from the merit of the Volunteers of Ireland. In asserting the independence
pendence

pendece of the Legiflature of Ireland, they were convinced they were promoting her happinefs and fecurity; they meant well, they acted nobly, but they have failed in fuccefs. The fecurity and happinefs of Ireland is at prefent fufpended. It does not appear that the continuance of a feparate Legiflature will reftore it. Some new arrangement muft be tried. If the Volunteers of Ireland armed for the happinefs of their country, they armed for a feparate Legiflature, provided they could obtain it; but if that has failed, and nothing but an Union can procure it, they armed for an Union; it was not the means but the end which was in their contemplation. To fecure the liberty and the property of their countrymen, to increafe the happinefs and profperity of their country, were their object; and whoever beft purfues that object, fights in their caufe, and enlifts under their banners. Can we fuppofe, if, in 1779, Ireland had been united to Great Britain by an identity of Legiflature, that if her privileges had been equally great, and equally eftablifhed; that if we had then been in the enjoyment of a trade as free as the commerce of England; if her liberties had been fecured by the Habeas Corpus Bill; if our Judges had been independent, and if we had not been degraded by Legiflating Privy Councils—in fhort, if our Conftitution had been the fame as the Britifh, that the Volunteers would have ftood forth to deftroy the profperity and happinefs of fuch a ftate, and have

diffolved

diffolved that which produced them? Would they not, on the contrary, have confidered any attempt to feparate the kingdoms as hoftile, and have treated the advifers of fuch folly as enemies?

Nor was it fo much the theoretic defects of our former connexion with Great Britain, which roufed the volunteers, as the practical evils refulting from it, and efpecially the reftraints upon our commerce. But their acquifitions, which removed thofe evils and reftraints, have produced, (as was at the time foretold) new inconveniencies and evils: What then is the ftate of the cafe? a fubordination of the Irifh Legiflature to the Britifh, has been experienced and fou ᴐ injurious; a feparate Legiflature has been tried, and proved inadequate to fecure our happinefs; an incorporation with the Britifh Parliament may ftill be reforted to, which promifes the fecurity of our fubordinate ftate, the advantages of our independent fituation, and is in theory preferable to both.

Fourth.—*Muft it not be the height of folly to part with the management of our own concerns for ever?*

The obvious anfwer is, that in a fair Legiflative Union with Great Britain we fhall retain as far as is neceffary, and not part with at all the management of our concerns. We fhall have Irifhmen in the originating Cabinet of Great Britain; we fhall shall have a number of Irish Representatives in proportion to our relative consequence, and in the Parliament of the Empire. Our affairs will be there discussed by our own Members, in the presence of the wiseft and freeft assembly which ever exifted, where our intereft is their intereft, our profperity their profperity, our power their aggrandizement, and where of courfe the anxiety of our welfare muft be as great in the British as in the Irish part of the Legiflature.

But this objection might as well be urged by Yorkshire, or any county in England as by Ireland. It will be faid the Members for Great Britain will out-number the Members for Ireland, as five to one; fo may Yorkshire complain that the Members for Great Britain are in proportion to the Members for Yorkshire as fifty to one.

The fame weak argument was advanced at the time of the Union for Scotland; it was then refuted in terms, it has fince been refuted by experience.

Fifth.—*A kingdom that fubjects its own Legiflature to the will of another kingdom, becomes its flave.* Let the pofition be granted, and let it be allowed that it is true, with refpect to an Union of defpotic countries; with regard to an Union of free countries it does not apply. For an Union, prefuppofing that the Legiſlature of the united empire is compoſed of numbers of repreſentatives, proportionate to its component parts, and that the laws to be made muſt attach generally and not partially, and that there is an identity of privileges and intereſts throughout the whole; it will follow, that ſo long as any part of the Union remains free, the whole will remain free. Who would deſire to have better ſecurity for his liberty than an Engliſhman poſſeſſes for his ? The liberties of the empire are at preſent maintained by a ſeparate body of repreſentatives for Great Britain, and a ſeparate body of repreſentatives for Ireland; how will either be endangered when a common body of repreſentatives ſhall be formed on a ſcheme of mutual intereſt for the joint preſervation of both ?

Sixth.—It is urged *that the preſent is a moſt improper time to agitate the queſtion, when the people are in ſuch a ſtate of irritation and turbulence, and the kingdom engaged in war.*

It may be argued on the other hand, that the preſent is the period moſt adapted for its diſcuſſion; for whilſt the feelings of our late misfortunes are freſh, it is natural that we ſhould be anxious to provide every ſafeguard againſt their recurrence, and that we ought not to adjourn the conſideration of our permanent ſafety to a caſual interval of peace,

peace, when a temporary enjoyment of tranquillity may render us indifferent and regardlefs.

As to a time of war, it is true, that the Volunteers took advantage of the embarraffments of Great Britain in the laft war, to affert the independence of our Parliament. It is likewife true, that the United Irifhmen in the prefent war have taken advantage of the fuppofed weaknefs of Great Britain to play the game of feparation. When, therefore, enemies of the empire take advantage of a time of war and embarraffment to effect its ruin, we fhould turn againft them their own game, and make ufe of a time of war to eftablifh its fecurity.

Seventh.—*The queftion of Union is beyond the power and competence of Parliament; a Houfe of Commons elected for eight years, cannot abolifh the Houfe of Commons for ever.*

This objection is eafily anfwered by confidering the end of Legiflative inftitutions, by which their competency is beft defined. The end for which Legiflature is eftablifhed by a free people is to maintain their property, to protect their characters, to fecure the liberty of their perfons, and to confult the convenience and happinefs of the people. Now if it be not poffible for a Legiflature to enfure thefe ends to its conftituents by preferving itfelf

8   feparate

feparate from another kingdom, and if by uniting itfelf with another kingdom, it is certain or
highly probable that their ends will be attained; it
follows, that were a Legiflature to refufe entertain-
ing fuch a queftion it would defert its duty, which
is the purfuit of the general good. That in the
difcuffion of the queftion the Legiflature ought to
liften to the opinion of the people is true, and it
will not act againft that opinion if univerfal; but
on the other hand, it ought not to be terrified by
the clamour of a few, and fhould be fatisfied by
general acquaintance.

If this argument had any real weight, we could
never have obtained the reformation, and the
eftablifhment of Proteftantifm; we could never
have procured the Revolution, and have changed
the line of hereditary fucceffion to the throne;
the Union of Scotland and England could not
have been entertained. It is a common maxim
in logic, that what proves too much, proves
nothing; and if this maxim is applicable to fubjects, where ftrict reafoning is required, it cannot
be excluded from political arguments, where
probabilites and experiences muft be reforted to,
and queftions are to be decided by the principles
of moral reafoning, not by mathematical precifion.

Eighth. — The arguments from national dignity, and national pride, have been obviated al-

H   ready;

ready; but as they will be repeatedly urged, as being eafy topics of declamation, another mode of rejecting them may be fuggefted.

Ireland, independent Ireland, has, at this moment, its commerce in all parts of the world, protected, without expence, by the Britifh Navy. Her fupplies for the year are chiefly raifed by the Britifh Minifter in England, on the faith of the Britifh Parliament; her country is protected from domeftic and foreign enemies, by forty thoufand Britifh troops, at the expence to Great Britain, of feven hundred thoufand pounds a-year. If her dignity and pride do not fuffer by receiving fuch affiftance and protection, how can they be injured, if fhe makes herfelf a part of that nation, incorporates her Legiflature into that of Great Britain, and converts that protection, which fhe now receives as favour, into a right?

Ninth. — *When Ireland was fubject to the controul of the Britifh Parliament, was fhe not kept down in a wretched ftate of penury, by the tyranny of Great Britain; and will fhe not be reduced to a fimilar ftate, by again fubjecting her reprefentative to theirs? Has not all the improvement of the kingdom arifen from the exertions of a free Legiflature; and fhall we confent to part with that power, which has been the only caufe of our profperity?*

This

This argument would have some weight if an Union were a state of subjection, from which it is essentially distinguished, as has been demonstrated before. The great advantage of an Union is, that it places Ireland on an equality with Great Britain, and prevents its subjection for ever. The vice of our former connexion with England was, that Great Britain made laws to bind Ireland, without binding herself at the same time, by the same laws. After an Union, partial laws cannot be made, where general interest is concerned; we shall have full security that the British United Parliament will never injure Ireland, because it must at the same time injure herself, and this is the best possible security.

It is certain, that since the independence of the Irish Legislature, our commerce has increased, but that has been effected by Great Britain admitting us to her Colony trade and by relaxing the Navigation Laws; and if the giving us some of the advantages of British Commerce, has been of such benefit already, what progress may we not expect, when all the advantages of the British Market, and British Commerce shall be secured to us for ever, which cannot fail to be the effect of an Union!

Tenth. —

Tenth.—*An Union muſt be our ruin or deſtruction ; all we want is a good ſteady Adminiſtration, wiſely and firmly conducted, and then all things will go well.*

Here we muſt aſk, what is meant by *a firm and ſteady Adminiſtration?* Does it mean ſuch an Adminiſtration as attends to the encreaſe of the nation in population, its advancement in agriculture, in manufactures, in wealth and proſperity? If that is intended, we have had the experience of it theſe twenty years; for it is univerſally admitted, that no country in the world ever made ſuch rapid advances as Ireland has done in theſe reſpects; yet, all her acceſſion of proſperity has been of no avail; diſcontent has kept pace with improvement, diſcord has grown up with our wealth, conſpiracy and rebellion have ſhot up with our proſperity.

What then is intended by a *ſteady and firm Adminiſtration?* Is it a determined, inflexible ſupport of Proteſtant Aſcendency, and a rigorous and indignant rejection of Catholic claims? Who will be a guarantee of that ſyſtem, and whom will it content? The Catholics will not acquieſce in its propriety. A party of Proteſtants in Ireland, term it unjuſt and abſurd; another party in England term it by fouler names; great leaders in oppoſition, poſſibly the future miniſters of England, may condemn it; and ſome members of the

7   Britiſh

British Cabinet are suppofed to be adverfe to it. Its ftability may reft upon accident, upon the death of a *fingle* character, upon the change of a Minifter, on the temper of a Lord Lieutenant; and the policy of this fyftem is much doubted by the people of England.

But perhaps a *firm and fteady Adminiftration* means Catholic Emancipation and Reform. Dr. M'Nevin, however, and the United Irifhmen, affure us, that thefe meafures are the certain introduction of Separation and Republicanifm, and that they were merely adopted with that view by the United Irifhmen. *Fas eft & ab hofte doceri.*

If then mere attention to agricultural and commercial profperity, and to general improvement, will not preferve good order, fubordination, and allegiance; if the power of maintaining Proteftant Afcendancy is uncertain, and the project of Catholic Emancipation and Reform is pregnant with danger, ought we to reject the confideration of a meafure with contumely and difdain, which places our Conftitution on the fame footing of fecurity as that of Great Britain, and holds out Britifh Principles, Britifh Honour, and Britifh Power, as the guarantee of our Liberties and Eftablifhments?

A few of the topics relating to an Union have been now difcuffed, and it is hoped they have been
difcuffed

difcuffed in fuch a manner as to prove that the fubjeft of an Union with Great Britain deferves the ferious and calm deliberation of every honeft man ; that it is not to be encountered by paffion, nor combated with arms.

An Union has this advantage — it may be our falvation ; it cannot be our ruin.

Equal liberty, equal privilege, with the people of Great Britain, guaranteed by a Parliament compofed from the Reprefentatives of both kingdoms, and upheld by the power of all the fubjeéts of the two iflands; in fhort, the confolidation of Great Britàin and Ireland into one kingdom, with one Conftitution, one King, one Law, one Religion, can never be the ruin of Ireland. It widens the foundation of our liberties, it advances our profpeéts of improvement, it ftrengthens the bafis of profperity in domeftic fecurity, and enfures our Imperial Independence by confolidating our power.

There may be prejudices to overcome ; there may be private interefts to manage and to compenfate; there may be the intrigues of our enemies to counteraét ; but if the nature of our fituation, our permanent and great interefts, demonftrate an Union to be falutary for our perpetual improvement, fecurity, and ftability, let us boldly follow where our reafon leads, though private intereft and

local

local prejudice, and hoftile intrigue, fhall attempt
to impede and arreft our progrefs.

The defign of what has been written is to re-
move any improper prepoffeffion againft an Union
in general ; the detail of the fubject has not been
entered upon. It may be obferved, however, that
the following points are fuppofed :

Firft.—The prefervation of the Proteftant religion and eftablifhment, as a fundamental article.

Second.—An equitable number of Peers and
Commoners, to fit in the Parliament of the Empire.

Third.—An equality of Rights and Privileges,
and a fair adjuftment of commerce.

Fourth.—An equitable arrangement as to reve-
nues, debts, and future taxes, fuitable to our fituation and powers.

Fifth.—The continuance of the civil adminiftration in Ireland, as it ftands at prefent accommodated
to the new fituation of the kingdom.

Sixth.—An arrangement for the Roman Catholic clergy, fo as to put an end, if poffible, to religious jealoufies, and to enfure the attachment of
that order of men to the ftate.

Seventh.

Seventh.—Some further provifion to the Diffenting clergy.

Eighth.—An arrangement with refpect to tithes.

It is furely poffible that all thefe points may be
properly adjufted, by wife and noble men, fo as to
prove upon the whole a rational and permanent
fyftem upon which we may fecurely clofe up our
interefts with thofe of Great Britain: But it would
be ufelefs to enter into the detail of any meafure,
fo long as the public mind fhould refufe to dif-
cufs its principle. If all advantages are to be re-
jected, becaufe they cannot be obtained but
through the medium of an Union; if we had
rather continue in turbulent infecurity, than be
united in profperity and happinefs with Great
Britain; and if we prefer adhering with tenacious
obftinacy to falfe notions of Pride, rather than
to cherifh the fentiments of true Independence,
the labour of detailed reafoning would be loft
and futile.

But as we truft the foregoing obfervations may
tend to incline every rational mind to a fair Exa-
mination and Enquiry, we may hereafter profit on
the difpofition and temper of the Public, and fug-
geft a fcheme for confideration, accompanied with
calculations and details.

. Some of the statements which have been made
in this publication, seem to have the tendency of
increasing Party Animosity; whereas the object of
the writer is to reconcile and extinguish them ; but
he knows not how to induce men to think rightly,
without making them see their situation and con-
fess it.

The premises which have been stated cannot be
controverted. If our situation be imputed to mal-
administration, who can secure us from its recurrence? If to the instability of affairs, who can in-
sure their future consistency? If to the prevalence
of the Protestant Monopoly, who can induce men
to relinquish what appeared to them the security for
their properties? If to the efforts of the Catholics,
who can force them to abandon their claims?

Is there not some settlement to be anxiously
wished for, which may lay these causes of discon-
tent asleep, and quiet them for ever? We have
been sufficiently distracted and harassed. We
have drank enough from the bitter cup of dis-
sension. Shall then any attempt to ensure tranquillity be the source of discord; shall the discussion of a plausible theory lead to passion and re-
sentment; and an honest attempt to allay the com-
motions of the State, and to settle its jarring
interests, be a provocation to new animosities and
fresh outrages?

I

The

The enemies of the empire have ftated, that Ireland can never be happy until fhe is feparated from England; it is the opinion of many of her friends, that fhe never can be truly happy till fhe is entirely united with England.

The one attempt would make Ireland the fcene of conteft in Europe; would deluge her with blood; would reduce her to defolation: the latter by making her power, the power of Great Britain, and the power of Great Britain her own, would enable the Britifh Empire to defy every hoftile attack, and to fecure to the happy coafts of the two iflands, all the bleffings of genuine and rational liberty, of true and folid independence and fecurity.

THE END.

www.ingramcontent.com/pod-product-compliance
Lightning Source LLC
Chambersburg PA
CBHW022155020726
47496CB00008B/2734